KATHLEEN FRASCONA

BEAUTIFULLY BROKEN

"Create YOUR beauty out of YOUR brokenness"

Kathleen Frascona

"Beautifully Broken" is unedited.

It is written through raw, racing memories, tear burnt eyes, fear, exhaustion, nausea, suffocation, and anguish.

Thank you to everyone who has supported me, cared for me, loved me, forgave me.

I am Proof ~~ You CAN and WILL Survive!

Kathleen Frascona

Beautifully Broken

I am alone in my thoughts
What will they say
Crashing
Falling
Make it through another day
Hurting, broken, lonely, lost
Giving up, giving in, losing all hope

Saying goodbye, what does it mean
Shadows of footsteps
Emotional scream
Deafening silence or
Blinding darkness
Nightmare or dream

I'm not a superstar or someone famous with a tragic story, I am the girl next door that everyone ignored.

Kathleen Frascona

I wrote this for you -

> You who sits in the corner, alone.
>
> You who cries in the shower.
>
> You who is to terrified to speak.
>
> You who feels shame.
>
> You who are in fear.
>
> You who sits in silence.
>
> You who are lonely.
>
> You who wakes in panic.
>
> You who trembles.
>
> You who screams.
>
> You who fall.
>
> You who feels worthless.
>
> You who feels abandoned.
>
> You who suffocates under the forced smile.

YOU

I met me today ~ confused, scared, lonely, frightened, hurt and abandoned me.

I looked into that shattered mirror and realized that was me, shattered. I spoke to that shattered mirror with such anger, hate, disgust, pity, shame —I had nothing to offer, no forgiveness.

I became a shell of myself, but how do you become a shell of something you never knew?

I wanted to write something brilliant, poignant and earth shattering ~

But then I wondered who would care?

> Who would listen?
>
> Who would I help?
>
> Who would read?

The journal I am writing this in was given to me by the most amazing girlfriends a girl could have. They wrote beautiful notes on the pages, notes that made me feel inspired, giggle, cry, feel loved—even if for just a moment.

I was told so many times, throughout my life, of how worthless I was, and am, and so much worse that I truly never believed that I have the love and support of my friends ~ I became my own worse enemy.

One of my favorite verses from the Bible is Psalm 139:14, "I praise You because I am fearfully and wonderfully made; Your works are wonderful, I know that full well." I pretended that was for me. Yet in reality, it was another lie I told myself. There was no way that verse was meant for me. Where was He to protect me? Why did He abandon me? Why didn't He just let me die?

Empty, abandoned, confused, lonely, unloved, scared, scarred, hated, used, shamed, abused—WHY?!

Part 1

Growing up was difficult, I barely remember anything happy.

I was abused - there, I said it!

Growing up, I was told I was "so damn fat and ugly that I'd better be smart because no one is going to want me".

The same person who told me this beat me, molested me, raped me.

I remember one day when he stormed down the hall, naked, angry.

He grabbed me by the throat, slammed me against the wall and started hitting me. I was so scared, I pee'd myself. When he was done, he threw me to the floor, told me I smelled like a whore and to go wash myself.

That was not the first or last time...

Have I ever told you that I am afraid of the dark? That's where the monsters are, or so I thought.

They are also in the light. They pretend that they are caring, wonderful, loving, and protective ~ and the world believes them.

"Eat your fucking eggs or I'm going to shove them down your God damned throat" - the eggs were undercooked, the whites were slimy, I vomited in my mouth and he made me swallow everything—eggs and vomit.

Mental, physical, and emotional abuse—everyday.

"If you tell anyone, I'll cut your tongue out and I'll cut out your mother's heart!" —- So, I kept my silence.

I got used to the beatings, they happened when no one was around, I knew how to hide them. I would suck my two middle fingers and tug on my right ear, I guess that was how I pacified myself?? I still cried, I shook in terror, wet myself—I was afraid, every minute, every day, I. Was. Afraid! But, I never showed it, I was always afraid of him killing my mommy.

The beatings turned into molesting. He'd follow me down the hall to my bedroom, I tried shutting the door but he would shove it open.

"This is going to hurt, but you're going to like it!" "You know you're trash and you deserve this!" is what he would say to me as he threw me on my bed, slid the crotch of my shorts over and shoved his fingers inside me. He would cover my mouth and nose with his right hand, no one could hear my scream. My tears burned my eyes, I couldn't breathe, I wanted to die— I was a student at Walsingham Elementary School.

The beatings and molesting continued for years, the molesting turned into rape. I lost track of how many times. I couldn't breathe, he always covered my nose and mouth, I couldn't see through my tears and clenched eyelids.

I learned how to pretend everything was good. There are many days I remind myself that I am "so damn fat and ugly that I'd better be smart because no-one is going to want me!"

I lost my childhood, my innocence - I lost me.

From Walsingham Elementary to Starkey Elementary —> From one abuse to another…

It was a new chapter but I still couldn't talk about me. I had no great stories, I was the broken girl who wanted friends, to be liked, to be loved—but kids are mean too…

My mother was great. She worked a full-time and a part-time job to take care of her children and our home. We did not have the best of everything but she did the best she could.

I wasn't physically attacked in Elementary school, I was verbally and emotionally attacked. Bullying has existed since the beginning of time and unfortunately it will never go away.

I was called names, made fun of, laughed at, mocked, notes telling me "I should not have been born" and "no one wants to be my friend". My clothes were ridiculed, my hair was always the joke. I smiled, kept moving, kept my chin up, and then cried in the bathroom.

You have to ask yourself what is going on in the home of the bully—that they could be so horrendous to another person? Was their family the same?

I had few friends.

I pretended to cheerlead during P.E., I broke records in the 50 and 100 yard dashes, received the Presidential Physical Fitness Aware, Honor Roll, and was part of the school safety patrol.

You see, I can pretend all things are good.

They just weren't...

Elementary school turned into Middle school.

Part 2

I don't remember much of Middle school, except that I liked to roller skate, I was pretty good too.

It's terrible to try to think back and see nothing but a complete blank. I try hard to remember things, but only blips appear.

I do remember missing my bus home one day, on purpose—I was being bullied on the bus. A friend of mine, J.C. offered to take me home. He was picked up in the family limo, I was truly grateful and embarrassed at the same time.

I do remember almost dying.

I was walking with a friend, I don't remember her name, we'll call her "Sherry"??? What we were doing, I don't remember, we were just walking along Seminole Boulevard.

I walked into the road, I don't remember doing it, I don't remember seeing anything, everything was blank. I remember hearing something, but it's like I wasn't there. Then, someone grabbed my right shoulder and I stopped in the middle of the street. A city bus sped by me, right in front of my face—it was then I came to. I was frozen for a moment, everything was in slow-motion, then I turned toward the sidewalk, to "Sherry" and screamed thank you—she DID NOT stop me, she was the noise I heard, she was screaming on the sidewalk.

I gathered myself and ran to safety. I was trembling, I couldn't stop rocking, back and forth on my feet. I asked "Sherry" who stopped me. She looked at me with wide eyes and said no one was there. I told her, "no, someone grabbed my right shoulder and stopped me in my tracks!" She just looked at me and shook her head.

I didn't understand it then but, as I got older, I knew **He** saved me.

I would frequently miss my bus to school so my mom would have to drop me off. I didn't want to tell her I was being bullied. I didn't want her to know that it was the daughter of one of her friends.

There was one day she caught up to me. She would constantly hit me in the head on the bus ride home, throw things at me, call me names, get others to join her—I never understood why, I didn't do anything to her or anyone else for that matter. We got off the bus, I started walking, quickly, home and she punched me in the head, I fell, my backpack went flying. I remember screaming "WHY?!" and she just said because. No one stopped her, everyone laughed and egged it on. I'm certain if we had cellphones, someone would have recorded it.

I made it home—bloody lip, ripped shirt, tears. I cleaned up before my mom got home — Everything was perfect, as always.

If it wasn't "friends" hurting me, it was also people "close" to me.

I remember visiting family. We were picked up at the airport and drove to their home. When we arrived, one of the women asked the man who picked us up, "How much did they offer you for her?" I didn't understand at that time. They both starting laughing— <u>he did not protect me.</u>

I was wearing a navy blue with white polka dots jumper, shorts/skirt. I had a set of long white glass pearls on, earrings and white "Florida" sandals. Apparently I looked like a hooker. I don't think I was 13 yet.

These were people who were supposed to protect me.

Roller skating was my safe place. Backward skate, bounce skate, speed skate—just skate, drown out everything except the music.

I was in my own world when I went skating. Boy did I think I was cool. We all did.

But, I was lonely, sometimes I would just sit on the large, carpeted boxes they had and watch everyone. I wanted a true friend. I would see the guys and girls slow skating and wish that was me. It wasn't and it's ok.

I would pretend everything was great and make up wonderful stories to tell.

Being told for so long how unloved and unworthy you are, you believe it. You wonder to yourself, "who would want to be my friend?" Why would anyone?

There comes a time in your life when you are supposed to figure out who you are.

That time was taken away from me. How do you figure out who you are when you are always told you are "NOTHING"!?!?

Sitting here now (2021) with tears running down my face.

Middle school turned to High school.

Part 3

I'm in high school now, I don't remember when it all came crashing down. High School was horrendous!

The students were horrible, I had few friends, mostly frenemies. I made terrible mistakes.

I wanted so desperately to be liked, to be loved, that I believed <u>anyone</u> who told me they did.

I never knew the real meaning, action, or truth in "being liked" or "being loved". I never had anyone to show me.

Being told, my entire life, that I was worthless, useless, a nothing, trash, shouldn't have been born, I should go kill myself, disgusting, no one wants you, no one likes you, fat, ugly, stupid, a disease, my mother should have gotten rid of me—I held (still hold) these internally.

You truly end up with no belief in yourself, no strength, no care, no like, no love, no nothing — you just — EXIST.

Oh to be popular…

I didn't look like the other girls, I wasn't skinny, tiny. I didn't have straight hair, I didn't wear fancy clothes.

So, I would get up every morning at 5:00AM, two and a half hours before school would start. I had to "get ready".

I would shower and then dry my hair straight, it took forever with the amount of natural curls I had. Everyone always made fun of my hair, called me a "cross-breed". Everyday I would wash my hair, use my hairdryer on high heat and pull through my hair a large round brush. Then I would use a curling iron to smooth out my hair and finally put "curls" or "height" wherever I wanted.

I still wasn't good enough.

I would vomit several times a day. After lunch at school, when I got home from school, after dinner. I couldn't gain weight, I was always trying to look like all the other girls.

There is no joy in trying to be like everyone else. I was a chameleon, I tried blending in...

I was taken advantage of.

High school is hard, any school is hard. Different cliques, different groups, different talk, different pain, different cruelty—"Mean Girls", "Mean Guys" have always existed.

I remember Senior year wanting to run for Student Government President. My posters were made and hung and some cruel people wrote over my name.

"Kathi Fr~~a~~cona for Class President"

FrASScona

So "**FrASScona**" is what they changed it to.

I was so angry with myself for never being able to stand up for myself. Why would I value something that no one else valued?.

Do I hold them accountable now? Girls were mean, I mean absolutely HORRIBLE! Guys used me, lied to me, took advantage of me, berated and belittled me—and I never stood up for myself.

No one knew of the abuse I suffered, no one cared. No one ever asked. Would I have said anything? Probably not, I lived my life in shame.

High school boys promise you the world and then they destroy you mentally, emotionally, verbally, and sometimes physically. "Have sex with me, if you don't, I'll tell everyone you did anyway!"

By the way, I was date raped, **twice**, but who would believe me? Not one person cared enough—not even me.

To be honest, I had a couple of good friends—they were exchange students. And I had one person, who, I now believe, truly loved me.

I was threatened so many times over the course of high school. I remember one day walking into typing class, yes we had typing class, and "JL" someone who I thought was a friend made a motion to another student to advise her I was walking in class. I sat down and this girl got up screaming at me, threatening me because I "flipped her off" for her flashing her high beams at me.

Apparently I'm driving home from work one evening and she gets behind my car and flashes her high beams. I had no idea who it was, I was in the right hand lane, going the speed limit and she flashes her high beams. So I casually put my middle finger up in the rear-view mirror and I kept driving.

Instead of acknowledging what she did, she proceeded to threaten me. Everyone laughed, "Fight! Fight!", "I'm going to kick your ass!"

I wanted to die so many times, I was just too much of a coward to do anything to myself.

I have hated myself for my entire life. I look into the mirror disgusted at what looks back at me.

I am that person they laughed about, talked about, threatened, abused, ignored… That is me.

"Here lies Kathi, her mind and body fried, she couldn't get the right hair color so she just curled up and dyed"

I may have been "fried",

but what was your part in my pain!

Not every part of high school was horrible, but enough of it was and that's all the memories I have…

Part 4

I couldn't wait to get out of Florida. The further, the better.

I was happy, I thought I was happy. I was staying with friends in Monterey, California.

I was still lonely…

I met people, went out, had nice times.

I got the "I don't know what I want to do in college" job, jobs. I traveled around California, drove down to Mexico, and over to Nevada, Arizona, and New Mexico.

I met "him". We spent so much time together, slowly getting to know each other, laughing, talking—and then one night we were sitting on a swing set and he said, "I'm going to marry you!" - I busted out laughing. I felt horrible, but I couldn't stop laughing. And then I said, "yea right!"

We had good times, we had bad times—ups & downs.

It's difficult when you lose track of time, timelines. Everything good that happened to me in California just fell apart.

We were dating, we were engaged and then it began…

His family made the beginning "niceties". We had "family meals", went to "family events" - I was even dressed in beautiful sarees, shalwar kameez, lenghas, and even wore bindis.

I will admit, his aunt and cousins were some of the most beautiful souls I have ever met. Kind, caring, compassionate, never an ulterior motive.

My memories of his parents are horrible nightmares. Again, I wasn't good enough. His mother would call me "white trash, whore, dirty, and other things in Hindi that I did not understand", she would call me and tell me to "leave her son because if I don't, they will disown him!" She reminded me several times that "I was not good enough for her son and his life would be better without me".

I pushed on and pressed on, was I proving them wrong or me wrong? Then it happened, I got pregnant. I was **so very sick**, couldn't eat, barely move, spotting—a lot and I was staying with his aunt and cousins.

His mother phoned me every day, several times a day. She would threaten me on the phone. She said she cursed me with illness and death, my child would never be welcome. How much of it did I believe? How much of her hate and vulgar influenced me?

And then it happened…

He looked at me one day and said, "My mother is right, it's a mistake to have this baby." That night, I bled and the pain reached every fiber in my body.

Everything stopped.

I have no recollection of what happened after he said that to me and before my doctor appointment. What I do remember is my doctor trying to console me. My body wasn't "holding" my baby anymore —it was now considered a "non-viable" pregnancy.

He was gone.

We still got married, I tried to pretend, I tried to make everything alright.

I waited long enough, until I felt "healed enough" to go back to Florida.

We were in Florida for a while, working, had a nice apartment, just going through life. There are so many memories blocked out.

Then she called, his mother. His father was not doing well and she needed him back in California. I didn't want to go, he said he wouldn't go if I didn't come with him. I caved, I went.

When we arrived it started all over again, yet was worse.

I was not welcome in their home, she would not allow me to "dirty her home". I looked at her and told her, "he would not be here if it wasn't for me!" — and then, she threatened to poison me.

Que after que after que was there, he never stood up for me, never fought back his parents, never demanded they stop. He ignored my pleas to go back to Florida.

His father threatened to kill me several times. He made sure to let me know that he would dump my body in the California desert and no one would ever find me.

One night he told me he was going to "beat my skull in" with a cast iron frying pan and saying "yes, he was going to kill me". The only other part of that night I remember is trying to escape through the second story window; my husband and his brother pulled me back in.

I don't remember when, but we went back to Florida. Things did not get better, I couldn't focus anymore, I tried, people believed all was well—but my nightmares were horrific.

Every night I was running for my life, and would wake up just before I died. My nightmares got worse. I would sleep and this beautiful, black haired, olive skin, big brown almond shaped eyed little boy would look at me and say, "Mommy, why did you let them kill me?!"

What good was I, I couldn't even protect my son and I couldn't kill myself, I was too much of a coward.

I was shattering, I was broken.

I had to get away.

Somehow, someway, I got the idea to move to South Florida and go back to school. I suggested we get a divorce, it would be easier for scholarships and grants.

We were 275 miles away from each other, divorced but not apart. We would visit each other, I guess hoping we could make it work—I already knew it wouldn't.

I re-started college but could never find my place. I went out, I worked out and I worked out and I worked out. I always thought I was too fat. Looking back at pictures, I looked like skin over bone.

Dates happened, nothing too serious. I was confused, didn't know where, or if, I belonged, just existing and pretending everything was fabulous.

I even dated a famous football player's brother for a R E A L L Y short time… I remember telling him I was going to see my Mom, he said I couldn't go and if I did, "not to come back." I walked out, shut the door and never looked back.

That was the first time I stood up for me!

Welcome to Miami— Bienvenido a Miami.

Yes, Miami was everything everyone thought it was...

Beach, Clubs, Dancing, Food, Drinks—a constant overload. There were beautiful people everywhere.

I still was not comfortable in my own skin, but I did try to blend in — the chameleon effect...

I had a little part-time job with a major beverage company. I was paid bigtime for being a "shot girl". I was invited to all the best clubs, met so many people, I was literally never alone but I was incredibly lonely.

People knew me but no-one really knew me. I didn't even know me.

Life was a blur. A constantly moving, crowded, loud, lonely blur...

Do you remember who you were before...?

I don't remember who I was "before", I never even knew who I was.

This feels like the weirdest thing I've ever said to myself, but it is true.

How do I get to know myself?

It's said that it takes time to truly get to know   others, how long do we take to truly get to know ourselves???

Who am I???

Then, I met someone. We hit it off, no pressures, he had me believe that "plain Jane, boring me was good enough." Hell, I even believed it. Maybe I just didn't want to be alone.

Things started changing. He would say "try it one time, if you don't like it, you don't have to do it again." - That was NEVER true. He would push and push, it didn't matter how uncomfortable I was, gaslighting became an everyday occurrence. If I didn't smile in "pictures", he would nastily say "oh forget it!" and then withhold emotionally from me—how quickly I would smile.

Things that never happened in the beginning were pressed upon daily. I began questioning myself, I gave up on myself — AGAIN! My first experience with "Gaslighting" and "Narcissism" before they were "popular".

He told me once to "go ask any doctor and they will tell me that I am not right!" — am I wrong? What's wrong with me!?!?!?!?!?!? According to the doctor, nothing—yet here I am on Zoloft.

"I've lived a life of silence out loud." - Me

I learned how to fall asleep during the stress—
I would take four (4) Ibuprofen PM, 50mg of melatonin, two (2) extra strength Benadryl, and drink a cup of chamomile tea.

To You,

I am sick and tired of being constantly reminded that you are just not happy with WHO I AM.

You never cared how uncomfortable you made me or how you would humiliate me in my own bed and out in public. You destroyed any enjoyment I had with sex. I panicked going to bed because I would never know what you were going to say, do, or want.

I asked you why you didn't show me who you really were, what you really wanted when we began dating, do you remember what you said???

You said you didn't show me because you "didn't want to scare me away." **It took me a long time to stand up for myself.**

Part 5
The "Ad" that changed my life

I needed to do something different for myself, I needed to like who was looking back at me in the mirror.

I saw an ad for a medical staffing agency and decided to apply. It was one of the best decisions I ever made. I went in for a Medical Assistant interview with an Orthopedic office and that's where I met Jen. She was interviewing for her position as she was being promoted. I always joked that I took her job and got a BEST FRIEND out of it too. We have been friends for the last 26 (and counting) years.

We have been together for the ups and downs, the laughter and tears. We were together for weddings, divorces, new careers, new homes, and babies.

We grew…

At 26 I met my future husband.

There he was, leaning over the engine of a car he was working on and I thought, "what a cute butt". Then he stood up. "What a cute face too!"

Introductions were made, a goofing off connection happened. We would chat every once in a while, poke fun at each other and one day, I decided to ask him out—I got tired waiting for him.

I took a deep breath and called him, the entire time I am whispering, "please don't answer, please don't answer." - He answered.

Gulp!

Welcome to the stuttering, stumbling conversation and the ending of: "would you like to go out with me one night?" His response: "YES!"

October 1996 was our first date. We had a wonderful dinner and an even better conversation. We talked for hours, there was no awkward silence. There no rushing, just talking and laughing and laughing and talking.

I asked him why he didn't ask me out…….

He said he thought that I was "out of his league." Let the blushing begin.

We began dating and like every couple, there were good times and rough times - we worked through them.

He owned a 4-plex in Coral Springs and eventually I decided to rent a 2 bedroom unit from him. Yes, I was his girlfriend, but I was also responsible. We talked about living together and I said not unless we were married. That was a short-lived idea. You see, the fear and trauma was coming back into my life.

Coral Springs, Florida was known as the "Blue Ribbon" Community for Families. It's the place where you are supposed to feel safe.

Monsters aren't always in the dark.

I was getting ready one afternoon, Mike and I were going out for the day. I got out of the shower, robe on and towel around my head and I hear a knock on the door. I walked to the door and there was a knock again - it didn't sound familiar. I said, "Mike, is that you?" The voice said, "yeah babe, it's me". The voice was gruff and mumbled, I asked again and got the same reply. I knew it was not Mike. I backed away from the front door and began banging on the hallway wall, Mike's apartment was right above mine. Within 30 seconds I heard banging on my door, it was Dave, Mike's roommate. I told him what happened and he ran upstairs to get Mike (he was in the shower). Mike and Dave ran downstairs and each ran in opposite directions around the building. Out of the corner of his eye, Mike noticed a sparkle/light bounce in the bushes. A guy ran out of the bushes and towards the front of the unit. Mike tackled him and proceeded to choke the gut with the strap of the camcorder he had. The Coral Springs Police showed up. They thanked Mike and told him he should be an officer. The guy was arrested.

The Coral Springs Police Officers went through the guy's bag. He had duct tape, rope, a knife, and his camcorder. He was a registered sex offender.

I am thankful for the thorough investigation by The Coral Springs Police Department. When they searched his apartment, he had an entire wall of pictures of me. I was violated - again. With their investigation wrapping up, they said they had enough evidence and I did not have to go to court. I was relieved. He went to prison.

Mike said he was moving me in with him. He was so afraid that someone would take me out of his life. I agreed.

Valentine's Day 1998, Mike proposed.

We were that "cool couple" at Dave & Busters, eating food and playing video games. He had a present for me - the box, inside a box, inside a box type gift.

Inside the 4th box was a little box and inside the little box was my engagement ring. He asked, I said "YES!" He told me that he had been carrying my engagement around in his wallet for months.

The Manager of Dave & Buster's saw us and brought over a bottle of champagne to celebrate. Our wedding was May 22, 1999.

Welcome to Newly Wed life…

Would I be able to have a family? I had already had two miscarriages. April 2000, I had my third miscarriage. I was at work, doubled over, fell, and passed out. I woke up in the hospital. Depression set in, I couldn't stop crying, what was wrong with me. I couldn't be happy. A friend of my found out she was pregnant, I couldn't be happy for her. I was in anguish.

Mike tried to talk me through, he helped me to be happy for my friend - I just couldn't be happy for me.

August of 2000 I found out I was pregnant, again.

For the first three months of my pregnancy, I was on an IV drip. I couldn't eat or drink, nothing stayed down. I was constantly sick and spotting all the time. By month four I was put on bed rest. My body kept trying to "reject" my baby. Then they started the steroids. They were trying to build up my son's lungs. Steroids by mouth, steroids by injection - whatever they said to save my son.

My little fighter was not supposed to be born until the end of April 2001 - He decided he was not waiting any longer. I was brought to the hospital and induced on March 6, 2001.

A doctor came in to give me an epidural, he missed over and over, blood was all over my back and onto the bed. Mike threw him out. Less than an hour later, another doctor came in. He assured Mike that he would not miss.

Everything was a blur and then I heard "Don't tell her!" Then my eyes closed. I don't know how much time passed but when I opened my eyes, they were handing me my absolutely wonderful, strong, beautiful, precious angel. His name is fitting:

Maico Angelos - he was protected by and named after the Archangel Michael, just spelled his name a little different.

Family, friends, so many people showed up to meet my little guy. I was so happy, so in love - so very protective. I had to protect him from the type of childhood I had.

One day, out of the blue, I remembered hearing "don't tell her." I asked Mike why he said that. His eyes widened and he said, "you heard me?" I said yes, and for some reason I just remembered. He proceeded to tell me. Maico was blue and not breathing when he was born, the umbilical cord was wrapped around his neck. I was frozen, I couldn't breathe. I cried.

Doctor's appointments, check-ups, milestones, goals, everything was great. He was walking at eight months, talking at ten. He loved music and being read to, animals, peek-a-boo, bubbles, Church, playing, all the attention, yes, he was our little ham.

He grew and grew and before we knew it, school started. Memories of my childhood came rushing in. I was fearful.

I became that over-protective Mother. I spent the next 9 years as a Substitute Teacher with the School District of Palm Beach County. The pay was horrible, the growth, memories, and being with my son, through Middle and High School was wonderful.

I always prayed that Maico would not endure the ugliness and bullying that I went through. My prayers were not answered. No matter how cruel and horrible these children, and adults, were, he was still so kind and forgiving. When I met their parents, I saw where these kids got their behaviors from.

Middle School and High School were a little better, but unfortunately Maico decided to no longer trust people and creating friendships became difficult.

Seasons changed, life bloomed, I was still so afraid but I wanted to live, not just live, I wanted LIFE!

I wanted so many times to share my story with the world, to let others know that they are not alone but I never could. There was still the humiliation I lived with, the fear of rejection, the feeling of worthlessness and who would actually care about me!

Working in the school district, meeting so many students, I was able to somewhat find my voice. They, our youth, needed me. They would come to me when they felt no one would listen, I was "Ms. K" - I was there for them!

My trauma will live in me forever, I was nothing but collateral damage to demons—mine and others.

Even with writing this, I realize I am still holding back.

Part of me feels like I deserve to be cruel, hateful, ugly, and there are times I want to scream at people
~~~

[Why are you such a disgusting human being? Your behavior? Your attitude? Who do you think you are? I want to tell them that they are nothing except a waste of oxygen—but then I would be no better than they are.]

There is no regard for life, we see it everyday. No-one is taught how precious life is. Youth destroy other youth for fun, adults destroy other adults for fun, youth destroy adults, and adults destroy youth—FOR FUN! Lives are taken, lives are ruined and the ones who do it do not care.

Zero personal responsibility, zero accountability!

Where are you in creating a future worth living?

Are you at fault for hurting others?

Are you at fault for not protecting others? .

I've started and stopped writing my story so many times, I lost count. All I could ever see was humiliation, embarrassment, being judged, people still saying it's all my fault, and worst of all, nobody really caring.

It took my son, my amazing, wonderful, strong, caring, protective son to push me through. He said, "Mom, your story needs to be heard, people need to know they are not alone".

I remember overhearing him one day—we were at an event and he told a group of people, "My mom loves those that no one else wants to love".

Do you think he will ever know, or understand, how his words saved me?

Part 6
Life as an English lesson.

There were times I wasn't so nice. I don't know if I was trying to protect myself or give permission for my hurt and trauma to attack others?? What I do know, is it made me feel horrible. To those I hurt, I am sorry.

Because...

Life is a blip, somedays it's slow motion, other days it moves so quickly we don't remember it. But every part of it is important – and so are you. Ask yourself every day, "How am I raising myself?", "How am I raising those around me?"

Life was never promised to be anything – Life is ugly, sad, painful, destructive, broken, cruel – and yet, in all of that, the light will shine through the tiny slivers and cracks, showing you the beauty, the happiness, joy, love, kindness and light.

People are people, some are good, some are bad, some are kind, some are evil – Who are you in this great big world? I never knew who I was, I always made the joke about myself and used Julia Robert's character in Runaway Bride – do you remember the ending where she has a counter full of eggs and she is trying every one of them? She never knew how SHE LIKED HER EGGS... I never knew how I was supposed to like me or who I was...

I think it was then that I realized life is nothing but an English lesson.

There was no "special formula", no perfect outline, no step by step guide, no! Everything I needed to know could be summed up in "W, W, W, W, H, W".

My greatest wish for you is that you do not abuse yourself because you "don't fit into" the "worlds' fake, airbrushed outline"!

Who, What, When, Where, How, and Why...

Yes, it is really that simple.

Who.......

I never knew "who" I was, "who" I wanted to be, or "who" I was supposed to be. That was probably one of the biggest lessons I had to teach myself.

The hardest thing about "Who" is "What".

Everything could be worked on, repaired, and created by using:

Who
What
When
Where
How
Why

WHO did I want to be, WHAT did I want to be, WHEN in my life would I do it, WHERE in my life would I begin, HOW did I want MY Life, MY Future, MY Impact to look, and finally WHY? Everyday we are given the opportunity to CREATE ourselves; your choices, positive or negative, will determine your outcome.
#BeautifullyBroken ByKF

Our "Who" and our "What" are two different things. Your "Who" is your character. So many times, we'll confuse our "who" with our "what". Your "What" is what you do, what your talents are, etc.)

I remember hosting a motivational engagement and telling everyone that "you are who you are when you are in your car, alone, and your favorite song(s) come on. The minute the song is over, you look around, fix your hair, get out of your car, dust yourself off, straighten your outfit, look around again, and then become whatever it is society expects to see. We've been programed to be just that. –What's your favorite song / songs?

So many people looked at me, with wide eyes, as to say, "Oh my goodness, you're right".

So, now you take a moment, think about your favorite song / songs — who are you when they are on and there is no-one else is around?

Before I started to understand myself, I allowed my "Who" to make me a "pleaser" – I am so worried about what others think, say, and feel about me that I don't care about what I say, think, or feel about myself – it took me a long time to undo this, and it's not truly gone away.

Because of what happened to me, what I endured, I chose to become what everyone else wanted, needed, desired, demanded – it was easier than trying to figure out who I was. I made it easy for others to abuse me, I accepted it; yes it was out of fear, fear of me not liking the real me looking back at me through the mirror and what I didn't realize was how much I would hate myself for what I became through the demands and abuse of others.

As I got older, I began asking myself, "Who are they, what is it, with them, that I'm allowing to be my determining factor? Why am I giving away power over my life"? "Why am I answering them?"

Why? BECAUSE

It is difficult leaving an abusive relationship.

Stockholm Syndrome

There's a saying that I truly love, and I want to share it with you.

"If you don't know where it is you want to go, how will you recognize it when you arrive?"

When we wake-up in the morning, where do we want to go? Is your work going where you want it to go? What about your life, your dreams, your goals? Do you allow your past or current upset and trouble to occupy your mind causing a diversion and sabotage you?

Reality is, many of us live lives that were, and still are, damaged by others. We can continue to blame our lives on everyone and everything else—Reality is, That's Life! If I let my past consume me, I would have given up a long time ago. Now, I use my past to help others. Does that mean all my days are perfect? NOPE!

Decide.

Stop looking at your life with what you think everyone and everything else can bring to your table ~~ It's YOUR table! Who will YOU invite? What will YOU offer? How do YOU want YOUR table (life) to be?

I Decide Me!

And yes, You Can Decide You!

You must ask yourself the questions that are waiting in the back of your mind. You know what you want; you know where want to be and you just feel afraid to break thess destructive processes you live over and over? If what is close to you is not adding value to your life have the courage to distance yourself from it. More times than not, we stay because we feel "safe" ~~ now it's time to change…

You have spent years walking in your shoes, the advice you have for yourself is priceless.

Use YOUR advice and cultivate an environment that inspires you because you can be your greatest asset or greatest liability. Look within you, be intentional and make every action count. What will you do when you realize there are no limits on your life?

No limits!

Even through our damage, we all have the desire to have better than what we have; what we choose to do about it is what defines us.

I begin each day thinking about this and I apply the "D's" ~~ I <u>distance</u> myself from any <u>disruption</u> or <u>distraction</u>. Most times we allow these disruptions and distractions to consume our lives, everything we do, everything we are, everything we want and need. Ultimately they will set, follow, and complete the course into destruction. You see, what you allow to define you will define your course of life. Are these disruptions and distractions worth destroying your life? What can you do and what will you do to put yourself in front of these?

Everyday we have the opportunity to redefine our lives.

Take time and "talk" to yourself. Are you where you want to be? Did you take a turn, from your past, that sent you in the wrong direction? Remember, no-one knows you better than <u>you</u>. You and only you can turn your "position" into the direction that is best for the life you intend yourself to have.

We've all had positive experiences and we've all had negative experiences, yet it seems to be the negatives that dominate our thoughts, feelings, and memories. Negatives stop us from taking a chance on ourselves. Negatives tell us we'll just fail, so not trying seems better than failing – right? But by not trying, by not taking a chance to redefine your life, you've failed.

Tell yourself why <u>you</u> are holding <u>you</u> back.

I've been through a lifetime of abuse (mental, emotional, physical, verbal, and sexual) from family, friends, frenemies, enemies, & strangers. I've been told: "Your dreams will never come true", "You will never "Be", I've been told that I need to just forget and finally, I've been hired, fired, lied to, lied about and used.

Always remember, People are people, some are good, some are bad, some are kind, some are evil – Who are you in this great big world?

I have been through more hurt than I care to admit and yet, I have a positive outlook, a great smile (some say infectious), I give my all, will always help, support, and believe in others – even if I find it difficult, most days, to believe in myself.

I am a true believer that you cannot possibly know how or what I am feeling if you have not been in <u>my shoes</u>. As for the person who coined the phrase "I'm OK, You're OK" ~~ you are out of your mind!

I am the girl next door that no-one

>   Cared for
>
>   Listened to
>
>   Loved

I will never know everything you have endured, but if I can help, I will.

In the back of my book, I listed a few songs that "speak to me". One of the songs is "More Beautiful You" by Jonny Diaz – I don't think he knows what this song means to me.

"Little girl fourteen flipping through a magazine
Says she wants to look that way
But her hair isn't straight, her body isn't fake
And she's always felt overweight
*This is what I was always told – I was "so damn fat and ugly that I'd better be smart because nobody is going to want me"

Well, little girl fourteen I wish that you could see
That beauty is within your heart
And you were made with such care, your skin, your body and your hair
Are perfect just the way they are
*Then why was everyone cruel to me?

There could never be a more beautiful you
Don't buy the lies, disguises and hoops, they make you jump through
You were made to fill a purpose that only you could do
So there could never be a more beautiful you

Little girl twenty-one the things that you've already done
Anything to get ahead
And you say you've got a man but He's got another plan
Only wants what you will do instead
*20, 21, 23, 24, 25 – whatever "he wanted" because I never believed in me

Well, little girl twenty-one you never thought that this would come
You starve yourself to play the part
But I can promise you there's a man whose love is true
And He'll treat you like the jewel you are
*I did starve myself, literally and figuratively – I starved myself of food and of emotions, feelings, the very essence of me. Starving is not just food.

There could never be a more beautiful you
Don't buy the lies, disguises, and hoops, they make you jump through
You were made to fill a purpose that only you could do
So there could never be a more beautiful you, more beautiful you
*I bought every lie, disguise, and hoop only to be abused again and again.

So turn around you're not too far
To back away be who you are
To change your path go another way
It's not too late, you can be saved
If you feel depressed with past regrets
The shameful nights hope to forget
Can disappear, they can all be washed away

By the one who's strong, can right your wrongs
Can rid your fears dry, all your tears
And change the way you look at this big world
He will take your dark distorted view
And with His light, He will show you truth
And again you'll see through the eyes of a little girl
*I will never get to "see through the eyes of a little girl"

That there could never be a more beautiful you
Don't buy the lies, disguises and hoops, they make you jump through
You were made to fill a purpose that only you could do
So there could never be a more beautiful you
There could never be a more beautiful you"
*And yet in my eyes, there will never be a beautiful me

Writer(s): Kate York, Jonny Diaz, Album: More Beautiful You

Artist: Jonny Diaz

This is your life

    This is your choice

        This is your chance

Your voice, your memories, your life - YOU - have so much to offer. Give yourself permission to speak up. You are free from being silenced, you are free being shammed, You Are Free!

I am proof ~ ~ You Can and Will Survive!

Now it's your turn, what is your W, W, W, W, H, W?

<u>WHO</u> do YOU want to be?
<u>WHAT</u> do YOU want to be?
<u>WHEN</u> in YOUR life would YOU begin?
<u>WHERE</u> in YOUR life would YOU begin?
<u>HOW</u> do YOU want YOU Life, YOU Future, YOUR Impact to look?
and finally
<u>WHY</u>?

Songs:

Beautiful, Beautiful —Francesca Battistelli

More Beautiful You—Jonny Diaz

God Only Knows—For King and Country

Do Something—Matthew West

Paper Sun—Def Leppard

Pocketful of Sunshine—Natasha Bedingfield

One Step At A Time—Jordan Sparks

Move, Keep Walking—Toby Mac

Set Fire to the Rain—Adele

Hold On To Me—Lauren Daigle

Fight Song — Rachel Platten

Truth Be Told — Matthew West

Look What You've Done — Tasha Layton

Tell Your Heart to Beat Again — Danny Gokey

You Are More—Tenth Avenue North

Lift Your Head Weary Sinner / Chains — Crowder

Chain Breaker — Zach Williams

Firework — Katy Perry

Roar — Katy Perry

My dear, precious friend,

I see you, I hear you, I am you.

You can, and will, climb your mountains, swim your oceans, withstand your storms and conquer your monsters—just take your first step. You were never meant to live in fear or be neglected, you my dear, were meant to thrive!

So often we speak to ourselves with such hatred. We neglect ourselves with our own words and thoughts, because we were "programmed" to do so. We can reprogram ourselves, we can create WHO we want to be and WHAT we want to do - You have that power!

Be, to yourself, everything you need. Bloom where you are. Where do you want your story to take you? You are your Author, use your mind, heart, and pen to create . Give yourself permission to "Be".

With unfailing love,

Kathleen

These Women mean the world to me

Carolyn Miller   Patty Dutcher
Jen McGuinness   Shari Zipp
Niki Mastros-Breitigan
Megan Swope   Nicolee Hiltz
Damaris Rodriguez
Susan Delgado   Holly Evans
Melissa Kaminski
Mia San Antonio-Silvetti
Earlene Dormer
Susan Copenhaver
Michelle Rivers   Kim Benjamin
Cher Poitevien   Trudy Stewart

There are times when we are so fortunate to find a group of women who lift you up, even when you can barely stand.

Strength
Love
Compassion
Guidance
Grace
Mercy
Beauty
#Flawsome

Made in the USA
Middletown, DE
05 March 2023

26063680R00040